This delightful, yet hard-hitting book, is filled with principles and ideas that will help you get the most out of life. We at Honor Books hope you will look to the sayings in this book as "a launching pad" for success in your life.

It's time to realize that you *don't wait for your ship to come in...you swim out to it!*

Don't Wait for Your Ship To Come In . . . Swim Out To Meet It!
ISBN 1-56292-058-8
Copyright © 1994 by John Mason
P. O. Box 162002
Altamonte Springs, FL 32716-2002

Published by Honor Books
P. O. Box 55388
Tulsa, OK 74155

Opportunity is missed by most
people because it is dressed in
overalls and looks like work.
– *Thomas Edison*

It is always better to fail
in doing something than
to excel in doing nothing.

People would worry less
about what others think
of them if they only realize
how seldom they do.

What most folks need is an alarm clock that will ring when it's time for them to rise to the occasion.

Good resolutions are like babies crying in church; they should be carried out immediately.

– Charles M. Sheldon

A bad habit never goes away by itself. It's always an undo-it-yourself project.
– *Abigail Van Buren*

Most people are willing to change,
not because they see the light, but
because they feel the heat.

The past should be a springboard,
not a hammock.
— *Edmond Burke*

The secret of success is to start from scratch and keep on scratching.

No man was ever honored for what he received. Honor has been the reward for what he gave.
— Calvin Coolidge

Criticizing another's garden doesn't keep the weeds out of your own.

Don't be content to be
the chip off the old block –
be the old block itself.
— *Winston Churchill*

No one is immune to problems.
Even the lion has to fight off flies.

Following the path of least
resistance is what makes
men and rivers crooked.
– *Larry Bielat*

Many of us have heard
opportunity knocking at
our door, but by the time we
unhooked the chain, pushed
back the bolt, turned two locks
and shut off the burglar alarm –
it was gone!

Your struggle may be lasting, but it is not everlasting.

Don't ask, "What if it doesn't work?" Ask instead, "What if it does?"

Never judge a person's horsepower by his exhaust.

Forgive your enemies – nothing
annoys them more.

With some people you spend an
evening; with others you invest it.

It's what you learn after you
know it all that counts.
– *John Wooden*

The best way to bring focus into your life is never to place a question mark where God has put a period.

There are a lot of ways to become a failure, but never taking a chance is the most successful.

A wise old owl sat on an oak,
The more he saw the
less he spoke;
The less he spoke the more
he heard;
Why aren't we like that
wise old bird?

– Edward H. Richards

In the presence of trouble,
some people grow wings;
others buy crutches.
– *Harold W. Ruoff*

God made you an original,
not a copy.

There is one thing stronger than all the armies in the world, and that is an idea whose time has come.

– *Victor Hugo*

Happiness is always an inside job.

Be like the steam kettle!
Though up to its neck in
hot water, it continues to sing.

Those who complain about the way the ball bounces are often the ones who dropped it.

Those who are given to white lies
soon become color blind.

When we do what we can,
God will do what we can't.

Don't die until you're dead.

It's the person who doesn't need a boss that's usually selected to be one.

Some temptations come to the industrious, but all temptations attack the idle.

– Charles Spurgeon

There are two kinds of men
who never amount to very
much: Those who cannot do
what they are told, and those
who can do nothing else.
— *Cyrus H.K. Curtis*

If what you did yesterday
still looks big to you, you
haven't done much today.
– *The Sunday School*

Many people seem to think that
opportunity means a chance to get
money without earning it.

Success is a matter of luck.
Ask any failure.

God's gifts are never loans;
they are always deposits.

A man can't make a place for
himself in the sun if he keeps
taking refuge under the family tree.

People are funny; they spend money they don't have to buy things they don't need to impress people they don't like.

By perseverance the snail
reached the ark.
– *Charles Haddon Spurgeon*

Fear and worry are interest paid
in advance on something you
may never own.

How many people do you
know who became successful
at something they hate?

A man who carries a cat
by the tail learns something
he can learn no other way.
– *Mark Twain*

The best helping hand you will ever
find is at the end of your own arm.

The nose of the bulldog
is slanted backwards so he
can continue to breathe
without letting go.
– *Winston Churchill*

⚓

Those who don't take chances
don't make advances. Even a
turtle doesn't get ahead unless
he sticks his neck out.

Remember that the faith to move
mountains always carries a pick.
— *Anonymous*

Always tell the truth,
and you never have to
remember what you said.
– *T.L. Osborn*

Don't spend a dollar's worth of time for ten cents worth of results.

Worry gives a small thing
a big shadow.
– *Swedish Proverb*

Noise produces nothing.
Often a hen who has merely
laid an egg cackles as though
she has laid an asteroid.
– *Mark Twain*

Remember: It's not what you have,
it's what you do with what you have
that makes all the difference.

Gain control of your time, and you
will gain control of your life.

A flawed diamond is more valuable than a perfect brick.

The future arrives an hour at a time.

Most winners are just
ex-losers who got mad.

You don't drown by falling
in the water; you drown
by staying there.
– *Edwin Louis Cole*

⚓

It is better to be alone than
in the wrong company.

If a thousand people say
something foolish, it's still foolish.
Truth is never dependent upon
consensus of opinion.

There is one guaranteed formula for failure, and that is to try to please everyone.

No obstacle will ever leave you the
way it found you.

Fear of becoming a has-been
keeps some people from
becoming anything.
– Eric Hoffer

Say no to many good ideas.
Say yes to the great ones.

If you don't have time to do
it right, when will you have
time to do it over?
— *Anonymous*

⚓

The last time you failed, did you
stop trying because you failed —
or did you fail because you
stopped trying?

If you were arrested for being kind, would there be enough evidence to convict you?

One person with passion is
greater than ninety-nine who
have only an interest.

It is better to die for something
than it is to live for nothing.
– Dr. Bob Jones, Sr.

Said the robin to the sparrow, I
should really like to know why
these anxious human beings rush
about and worry so. Said the
sparrow to the robin, I think that
it must be they have no Heavenly
Father such as cares for you and me.

– Old poem in The Prairie Pastor

In the confrontation between the stream and the rock, the stream always wins – not through strength but through perseverance.

A genius is someone who shoots at a target no one else sees and hits it.

Dissatisfaction and discouragement are not caused by the absence of things but the absence of vision.

Worry is a darkroom where
negatives are developed.

When people are free to do
as they please, they usually
imitate each other.
– Eric Hoffer

It ain't no use putting up your umbrella till it rains.
— *Alice Caldwell Rice*

You're like a teabag – not worth much till you've been through some hot water.

Nothing dies quicker than a new idea in a closed mind.

The average man does not
know what to do with his
life, yet wants another one
which will last forever.

– Anatold France

⚓

It is not the man with a
motive but the man with a
purpose who prevails.

The only difference between a rut
and a grave is the timing.

Don't grumble because
you don't have what you want;
be thankful you don't get
what you deserve.

Some people stay so far
in the past that the future
is gone before they get there.

He who is afraid of doing
too much always does too little.

Brethren, be great believers.
Little faith will bring your souls
to heaven, but great faith will
bring heaven to your souls.
— *Charles Spurgeon*

⚓

When you can't change the
direction of the wind,
adjust your sails.
— *Max DePree*

Success is largely a matter of
holding on after others have let go.

Jealousy is the tribute mediocrity pays to achievers.

An obstinate man does not hold opinions – they hold him.

Don't dream up thousands of reasons why you can't do what you want to; find one reason why you can.

Little men with little minds and little imaginations go through life in little ruts, smugly resisting all changes which would jar their little worlds.

– Anonymous

When you help someone up
a mountain, you'll find yourself
close to the summit too.

Of all sad words of tongue
or pen, the saddest are these:
"It might have been!"
– John Greenleaf Whittier

I am only one, but still I am one. I cannot do everything, but still I can do something; I will not refuse to do the something I can do.
– *Helen Keller*

Your friends will stretch your vision
or choke your dream.

Today I will...Not lose an hour
in the morning and spend
all day looking for it.

Some people speak from experience; others, from experience, don't speak.

There is never a right time
to do the wrong thing.

Patting a fellow on the back
is the best way to get a chip
off his shoulder.

Even a fly doesn't get a slap on the back until he starts to work.

Remember, if you try to go it alone, then the fence that shuts others out shuts you in.

Attention men: Before you criticize another, look closely at your sister's brother!

When you're a self-starter,
others don't have to be a crank.

The person who really wants
to do something finds a way;
the other finds an excuse.

Show me a thoroughly satisfied
man, and I will show you a failure.
– *Thomas Edison*

An excuse is a thin slice
of falsehood stretched
tightly over a boldface lie.

Watch for big problems; they
disguise big opportunities.

Start with what you can do; don't
stop because of what you can't do.

Seek God first and the things you want will seek you.

A definition of "mediocrity": best of the worst and worst of the best.

The reason some people don't go very far in life is because they sidestep opportunity and shake hands with procrastination.

There is only one degree
of difference between
hot water and steam.

Everything big starts with
something little.

The only sure way to fend off
criticism is to do nothing and
be nothing. Those who do
things inevitably stir up criticism.

It is more valuable to seek God's presence than to seek His presents.

A man without principle never
draws much interest.

Two things rob people of their
peace of mind: work unfinished
and work not yet begun.

People who never do any more
than they get paid for never get
paid for any more than they do.
— *Albert Hubbard*

A person is never what he ought
to be until he is doing what he
ought to be doing.

Grow where you are planted.
Begin to weave, and God
will give the thread.
– *German Proverb*

Happiness will never come
to those who fail to appreciate
what they already have.
Most people make the
mistake of looking too far
ahead for things close by.

You can't consistently perform in a manner that is inconsistent with the way you see yourself.
– *Zig Ziglar*

When you don't have a good reason for doing a thing, you have one good reason for letting it alone.

Do all the good you can,
In all the ways you can,
In all the places you can,
At all times you can,
To all people you can,
As long as you ever can.
– John Wesley

Love looks through a telescope;
envy, through a microscope.

Persistence is simply enjoying
the distance between the
fulfillment of God's promises.

Weak men are the slaves of what happens. Strong men are masters of what happens.
– *George Craig Stewart*

A complaining spirit is first a caller,
then a guest, and finally a master.

The block of granite which was an
obstacle in the pathway of the weak
becomes a stepping stone in the
pathway of the strong.
— *Thomas Carlisle*

Take a tip from your Creator –
your ears aren't made to shut,
but your mouth is!

The only people you should try to get even with are those who have helped you.

If people talk negatively about you, live so that no one will believe them.

No one ever stumbled
onto something big while
sitting down.

Happiness is a direction,
not a destination.

The strength of a man consists
in finding out the way God is
going, and going that way.
— *Henry Ward Beecher*

There is no better exercise for the heart than reaching down and lifting someone else up.

The biggest enemy of best is good.
If you're satisfied with what's good,
you'll never have what's best.

Go from knowing what
others believe to knowing
what you believe.

Man is that foolish creature
who tries to get even with
his enemies and ahead
of his friends.

A person may fail many times, but
he isn't a failure until he blames
somebody or something else.

Life's disappointments are
opportunity's hidden appointments.

Good intentions are like
checks that men try to draw
from a bank where they
have no account.

Success lies not in achieving what
you aim at but in aiming at what
you ought to achieve.

We should work to become,
not to acquire.

There are many things that will catch my eye, but there are only a few that catch my heart . . . it is those I consider to pursue.

– *Tim Redmond*

Only those who do not expect
anything are never disappointed.
Only those who never
try, never fail.

Every obstacle introduces
a person to himself.

This week take a few minutes
and send a note to those people
who reached out and greatly
affected your life. Also do
this: take a few minutes
and reach out to help
someone else get ahead.

Direction is a matter of fact;
ideas are a matter of opinion.

What we learn about another
person will always result in a
greater reward than what we
tell him about ourselves.

It's not the absence or the presence of problems that determines our peace of mind; it's the absence or the presence of God.

Look carefully at the closest
associations in your life,
for that is the direction
you are heading.

⚓

Here is the key to being free
from the stranglehold of past
failures and mistakes: learn the
lesson and forget the details.

There is no shortcut to success. If you keep your attention on learning the tricks of the trade, you will never learn the trade.

Yes and No are the two most important words that you will ever say. These are the two words that determine your destiny in life.

Never surrender your dream to noisy negatives.

Jumping at the first opportunity seldom leads to a happy landing.

A leader looks for opportunities
to find someone doing
something right.

Stop every day and look
at the size of God.

People can be divided into three groups: 1) Those who make things happen, 2) Those who watch things happen, and 3) Those who wonder what's happening.

It's when the fish opens
his mouth that he gets caught.

Small minds are the first to
condemn great ideas.

No problem is too large for God's intervention, and no person is too small for God's attention.

Some people find life an
empty dream because they
put nothing into it.

The road to success runs uphill,
so don't expect to break
any speed records.

When God prepares to do something wonderful, He begins with a difficulty. When He plans to do something very wonderful, He begins with an impossibility!

We become like those with whom we associate: "A mirror reflects a man's face, but what he is really like is shown by the kind of friends he chooses."
– *Proverbs 27:29 TLB*

Unforgiveness does a great deal more damage to the vessel in which it is stored than the object on which it is poured.

Prayer is the key to real success; we stand tallest when we are on our knees.

Silence is an environment in which great ideas are birthed.

Retreat to advance. Sometimes the most important and urgent thing we can do is get away to a peaceful and quiet place.

You draw nothing out
of the bank of life except
what you deposit in it.

Silence is the ultimate weapon of power; it is also one of the hardest arguments to dispute.

If you treat a person as he is, he will remain as he is. If you treat him for what he could be, he will become what he could be.

You can make more friends in two months by helping other people than you can in two years trying to get others to help you.

If God can get it through you,
God will give it to you.
— Pastor E.V. Hill

⚓

You can't get ahead when
you're trying to get even.

Working together is essential for success; even freckles would make a nice tan if they would get together.

Give me a man who sings at his work. That's the kind of people I want to hire!
– *Thomas Carlisle*

A smile is the shortest distance between two people.

Find something you love to do,
and you'll never have to work
another day in your life.
– *Harvey Mackay*

A conceited person never gets
anywhere because he thinks
he is already there.

Too many people avoid discovering
the secret of success because
deep down they suspect the
secret may be hard work.

Keep your face to the sunshine
and you cannot see the shadow.
– Helen Keller

When you stretch the truth,
watch out for the snap back.

A successful man continues to look
for work after he has found a job.

Sitting still and wishing makes
no person great; The Lord
sends the fishing, but you
must dig the bait.

– Anonymous

The creation of a thousand
forests is in one acorn.
— *Ralph Waldo Emerson*

The measure of a person's real
character is what he would do if he
knew he would never be found out.

It's a funny thing about life;
if you refuse to accept
anything but the best,
you very often get it.
— *Somerset Maugham*

⚓

When the past tries to
dominate your thoughts, let
your dreams ignite your day.

If at first you do succeed,
try something harder.

The difference between ordinary and extraordinary is that little extra.

– Zig Ziglar

Excuses are the nails used
to build a house of failure.

Man cannot discover new
oceans unless he has courage
to lose sight of the shore.
– *Anonymous*

Life is either a daring
adventure, or nothing.
– *Helen Keller*

Happiness is not a reward –
it is a consequence.
– *Robert Green Ingersoll*

God doesn't call us to be successful.
He calls us to be faithful.
– *Albert Hubbard*

Consider the postage stamp.
Its usefulness consists
in the ability to stick to
something until it gets there.
– *Josh Billings*

⚓

One half of knowing what you want is knowing what you must give up before you get it.

Don't consume your tomorrows feeding on your yesterdays.

Doubt sees the obstacles
Faith sees the way.
Doubt sees the darkest night
Faith sees the day
Doubt dreads to take a step
Faith soars on high.
Doubt questions "who believes?"
Faith answers, "I."

When a man is wrapped up
in himself, he makes a
pretty small package.
– *John Ruskin*

When I was young, I observed that
nine out of ten things I did were failures.
So I did ten times more work.
– *George Bernard Shaw*

Remember in the eyes of average people, average is always considered outstanding.

Live your life as an exclamation,
not an explanation.

Trying times are no time
to quit trying.

You cannot live a perfect
day without doing something
for someone who will never
be able to repay you.
– *John Wooden*

⚓

It's amazing the amount
of work you can get done
if you don't do anything else.

Those who bring sunshine
to the lives of others cannot
keep it from themselves.

– James Matthew Barrie

Don't complain. The wheel that squeaks the loudest often gets replaced.

Everybody is in favor of progress.
It's the change they don't like.

Right is right even if everyone
is against it, and wrong is wrong
even if everyone is for it.

Big shots are only little shots that keep shooting.
– Christopher Morley

Attempt something so fantastic
that unless God is in it, it is
destined for failure.

We cannot become what we need
to be by remaining what we are.

You can't walk backward into the future.

"Impossible" is a word found only
in the dictionary of fools.
– *Napoleon*

He who expects nothing
shall never be disappointed.

The best rose bush is not
the one with the fewest
thorns, but that which
bears the finest roses.

– Jerry Van Dyke

⚓

The tragedy of life is not that
it ends so soon, but that we
wait so long to begin it.

Both faith and fear may sail
into your harbor, but allow
only faith to drop anchor.

Ideas have a short shelf life –
that's why we must act
before the expiration date.

Even if you're on the right
track – you'll get run over
if you just sit there.
– *Arthur Godfrey*

Anybody who brags about what he
is going to do tomorrow probably
did the same thing yesterday.

Beware of those who stand aloof and greet each venture with reproof; the world would stop if things were run by men who say, "It can't be done."

Indecisive people are like a blind man looking in a dark room for a black cat that isn't there.

Procrastination is the ability to keep up with yesterday.

Opportunities can drop in
your lap if you have your lap
where opportunities drop.

Eyes that look are common.
Eyes that see are rare.
– J. Oswald Sanders

It's not the difference between
people that's the difficulty,
it's the indifference.

Do you say "our Father" on Sunday and then act like an orphan the rest of the week?